Copyright 2018 by Lauren Boehm Lynch

ISBN-13: 978-1719527828

ISBN-10: 1719527822

Published by Broken Road Farm Publishing www.laurenboehmlynch.com

First Publishing 2018

Book Photographs by: Lauren Boehm Lynch, Tim Lynch and Megan Boatright

Book Cover design by: Lauren Boehm Lynch

The Broken Road Farm Counting and Picture Book

Lauren Boehm Lynch

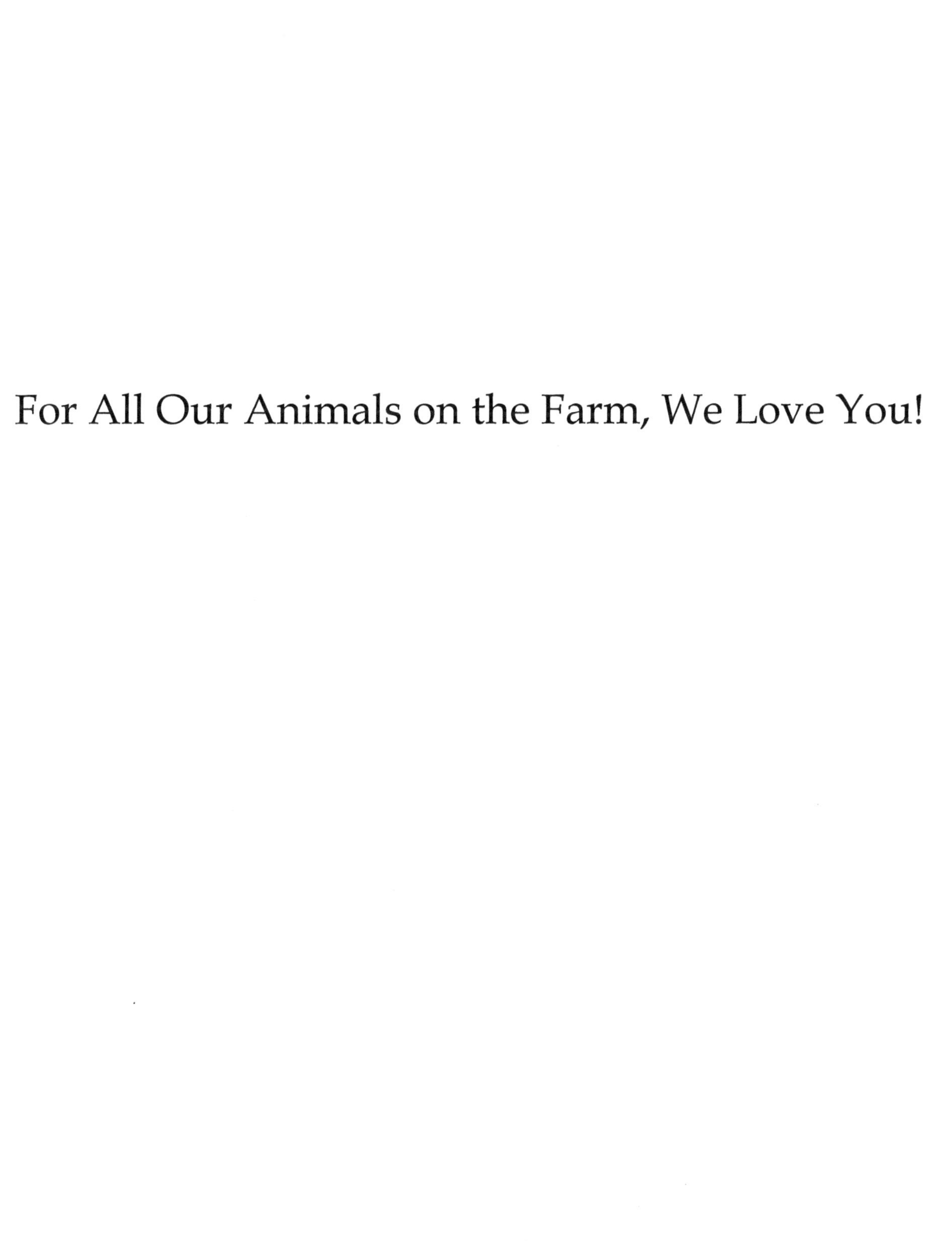

For All Our Animals on the Farm, We Love You!

2 Twin Baby Nubian Goats

1 Grey Farm Cat and 1 Calico Farm Cat

1 Momma Bird Peeping Out
of The Porch Birdhouse

Gigi Saying Hello

4 Nubian Baby Goats Playing on A Tub

Our Nubian Goat Herd

Trail Cam Took Picture of 2 Does

1 Goat Playing in The Field
with Tall Grass

1 Hen Waiting on Her Breakfast! Her name is Chicken!

1 Male Gobbler and 3 Female Hens

1 Male Gobbler Posing for The Camera

2 Male Ducks Chasing Chickens

1 Momma Pig and 3 Pink Piglets! There is a Black Piglet, can you find him?

This is Gladys the Opossum, she is in the cat's house. Guess she got cold!

1 Brown dog named Thorn and 3 Black dogs named Hoss, Moe and Whiner!

Lilly with 1 Grey Kitten and 2 Orange Kittens

Lucy Wishing you a Good Morning!

Ethel Wants A Kiss

How many Goats do you see in this picture?

Our trail cam took this picture of a Doe going to the feeder!

1 Hummingbird at The Feeder

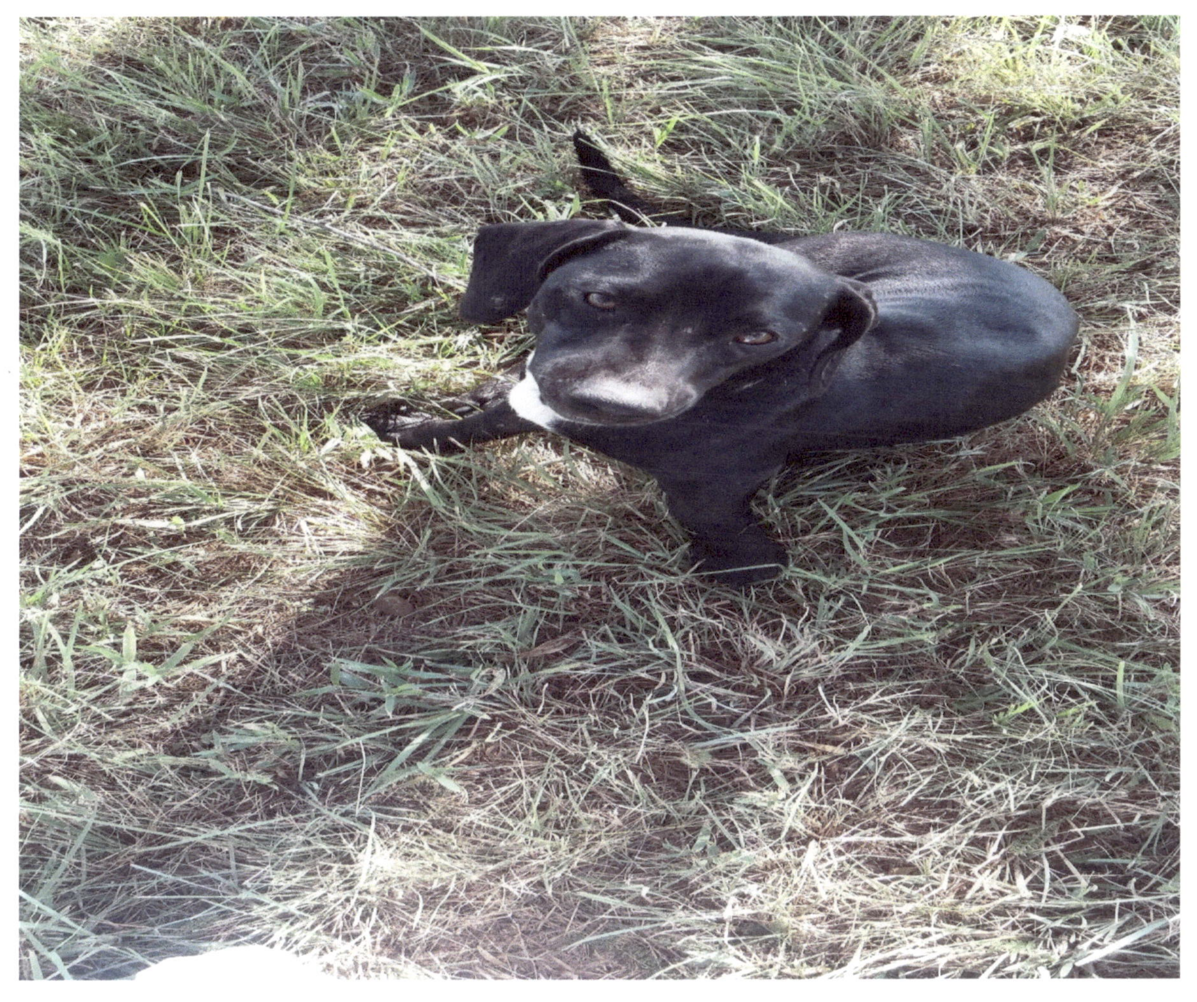

This is Hoss our Chi-Weenie dog, he loves to run and jump!

Lauren Boehm Lynch is a retired nurse living on the Broken Road Farm with her husband Tim and their many animals. The farm provides plenty of stories for her books.

www.laurenboehmlynch.com

www.facebook.com/AuthorLaurenBoehmLynch

www.ingramcontent.com/pod-product-compliance
Lightning Source LLC
Chambersburg PA
CBHW040037240726
48664CB00003B/971